Mary Jones, Diane Fellowes-Freeman and Michael Smyth

Cambridge Checkpoint

Science

Skills Builder Workbook

7

CAMBRIDGE
UNIVERSITY PRESS

CAMBRIDGE
UNIVERSITY PRESS

University Printing House, Cambridge CB2 8BS, United Kingdom

One Liberty Plaza, 20th Floor, New York, NY 10006, USA

477 Williamstown Road, Port Melbourne, VIC 3207, Australia

314–321, 3rd Floor, Plot 3, Splendor Forum, Jasola District Centre, New Delhi – 110025, India

79 Anson Road, #06–04/06, Singapore 079906

Cambridge University Press is part of the University of Cambridge.

It furthers the University's mission by disseminating knowledge in the pursuit of education, learning and research at the highest international levels of excellence.

www.cambridge.org
Information on this title: www.cambridge.org/9781316637180 (Paperback)

First published 2017

20 19 18 17 16 15 14 13 12 11 10 9

Printed in Great Britain by CPI Group (UK) Ltd, Croydon CR0 4YY

A catalogue record for this publication is available from the British Library

ISBN 978-1-316-63718-0 Paperback

Produced for Cambridge University Press by White-Thomson Publishing
www.wtpub.co.uk
Editor: Rachel Minay
Designer: Clare Nicholas

All Checkpoint-style questions and sample answers within this workbook are
written by the authors.

Acknowledgements

The authors and publishers acknowledge the following sources for photographs:

Cover Pal Hermansen/Steve Bloom Images/Alamy Stock Photo

....

Contents

Introduction

Welcome to the Cambridge Checkpoint Science Skills Builder Workbook 7

The Cambridge Checkpoint Science course covers the Cambridge Secondary 1 Science curriculum framework. The course is divided into three stages: 7, 8 and 9.

You should use this Skills Builder Workbook with Coursebook 7 and Workbook 7. This workbook does not cover all of the curriculum framework at stage 7; instead it gives you extra practice in key topics, focusing on those that are the most important, to improve your understanding and confidence.

The tasks will help you with scientific enquiry skills, such as planning investigations, drawing tables to record your results, and plotting graphs.

The workbook will also help you to use your knowledge to work out the answers to new questions.

As you work through the tasks in this Skills Builder Workbook you should find that you get better at these skills.

You could then try to complete some of the exercises in the Checkpoint Science Workbook.

If you get stuck with a task:

Read the question again and look carefully at any diagrams, to find any clues.

Look up any words you do not understand in the glossary at the back of the Checkpoint Science Coursebook, or in your dictionary.

Read through the matching section in the Coursebook. Look carefully at the diagrams there too.

Check the reference section at the back of the Coursebook. There is a lot of useful information there.

Introducing the learners

Nor   Amal   Sam

Anna   Elsa   Jon

1.1 Labelling a diagram of a plant

This exercise relates to **1.1 Plant organs** from the Coursebook.

> In this exercise, you practise labelling a diagram carefully.

This diagram shows a plant.

1 Add these labels to the correct parts of the plant.

roots   **stem**   **leaf**   **flower**

> ### Remember
>
> Use a ruler and pencil to draw your label lines.
>
> Make sure the end of the label line touches the part you want to label.
>
> Write the labels in the white space, not on the diagram.
>
> Try to keep your writing horizontal.

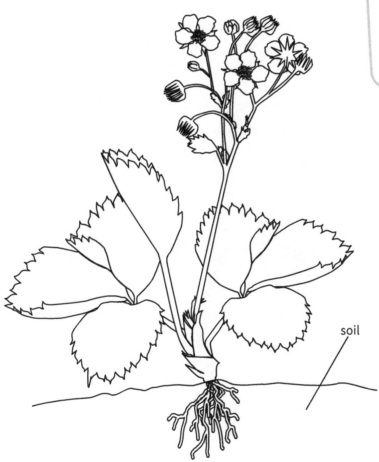

soil

1.2 Functions of human organs

This exercise relates to **1.2 Human organ systems** from the Coursebook.

In this exercise, you label some human organs with their functions. Follow the guidelines about labelling from exercise 1.1.

Here is a list of the **functions** of four of the organs that are shown in the diagram below.

- The .... pumps blood around the body.

- The .... coordinates actions of different parts of the body.

- The .... helps to digest food.

- The .... absorb oxygen from the air.

1 Use the list of functions to label the diagram. Complete each label by adding the name of the organ.

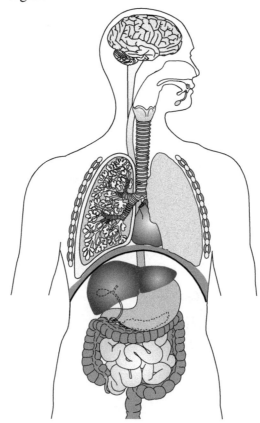

2 Now add at least one more label of your own. Your label should name the organ and describe its function.

1.3 The skeleton and forces

This exercise relates to **1.3 The human skeleton** from the Coursebook.

> In this exercise, you practise reading a scale and filling in a results table.

Sam does an experiment to measure how much force he can produce with his fingers.

He hooks a forcemeter to the bench.

Then he pulls on the forcemeter with the first finger of his right hand.

Here is a close-up of the scale on the forcemeter.

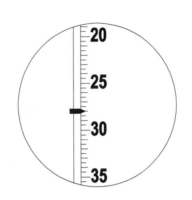

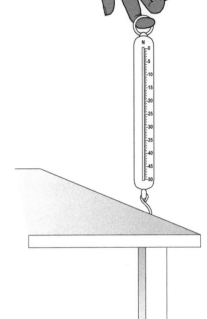

1 Who reads the scale correctly?
   Tick the box under the correct reading.

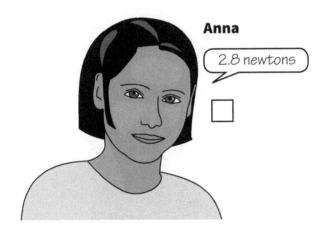

Anna
2.8 newtons

Nor
28 newtons

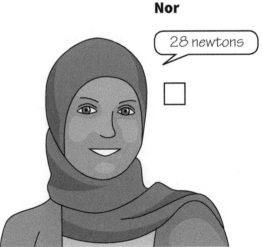

Amal
34 newtons

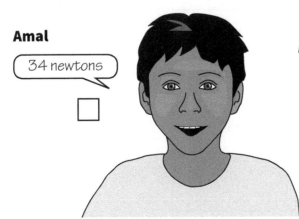

Sam now pulls the forcemeter with the thumb of his right hand, and then with his other three fingers.

These pictures show the forcemeter scale for each.

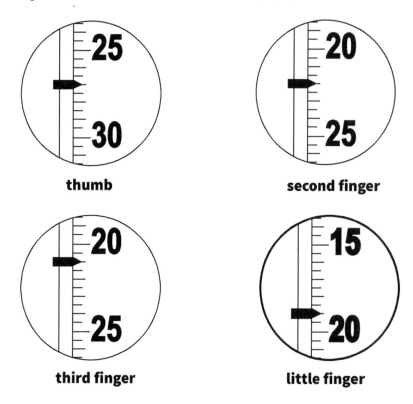

thumb	second finger

third finger	little finger

2 Write the readings in the correct spaces in Sam's results table. (The reading for Sam's first finger on his right hand is on the previous page.)

The results for his left hand are already completed.

	Force in N	
	Right hand	Left hand
thumb		25
first finger		25
second finger		19
third finger		16
little finger		17

Remember

N is the symbol for **newtons**.

The unit, N, is in the heading of the table, so you do not need to write it again.

1.4 Muscles experiment

This exercise relates to **1.5 Muscles** from the Coursebook.

In this exercise, you complete the headings and readings in a results chart. Then you think about making conclusions from a set of results.

Elsa wants to find out whether the muscles in her right hand or her left hand tire more quickly. Elsa and Anna do an experiment.

Elsa holds a clothes peg between the thumb and first finger of her right hand.

She uses the muscles in her thumb and finger to open and close the peg, as fast as she can.

In the girls' experiment, this is what they do:

- Elsa opens and closes the peg as many times as she can for five minutes.

- Anna uses the timer and counts the number of times Elsa does this in each minute.

Then they do it again, but this time Elsa holds the clothes peg in her left hand.

Here are the results that Anna writes down:

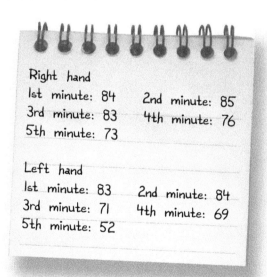

Right hand
1st minute: 84   2nd minute: 85
3rd minute: 83   4th minute: 76
5th minute: 73

Left hand
1st minute: 83   2nd minute: 84
3rd minute: 71   4th minute: 69
5th minute: 52

1 Complete the results table for Elsa's and Anna's experiment.

Time in	Number of times clothes peg was opened and closed	
	.... hand	.... hand
1		
2		

2 Elsa and Anna make some **conclusions** from their results. Tick the **one** conclusion that is correct.

Remember

A conclusion is something that you can work out from your results.

Do not use any information other than your results to make a conclusion.

Elsa is right-handed. ☐

The muscles in the left hand of a right-handed person tire more quickly than the muscles in the right hand. ☐

The muscles in Elsa's left hand tire more quickly than the muscles in her right hand. ☐

The muscles in Elsa's thumb are stronger than the muscles in her little finger. ☐

The muscles in girls' hands are not as strong as the muscles in boys' hands. ☐

Unit 2 Cells and organisms

2.1 Micro-organisms experiment

This exercise relates to **2.2 Micro-organisms** and **2.3 Micro-organisms and decay** from the Coursebook.

> In this exercise, you practise following instructions. You also think about variables in an experiment.

Jon does an experiment to compare the number of micro-organisms in the air in Classroom 203 and Classroom 204.

These are the instructions that the teacher gives Jon for Classroom 203.

1. Collect a dish containing sterile agar jelly.

2. Label the base of each dish with the number or name of the classroom you are testing.

3. Place the dish in the classroom and take the lid off.

4. After five minutes, put the lid back on again.

5. Use a small strip of tape to stick the lid onto the base.

6. Place the dish, upside down, in a safe place in the laboratory.

The pictures on the right show Jon following the instructions. They are not in the correct order.

1 Write a number in the box next to each picture to show which instruction Jon is carrying out.

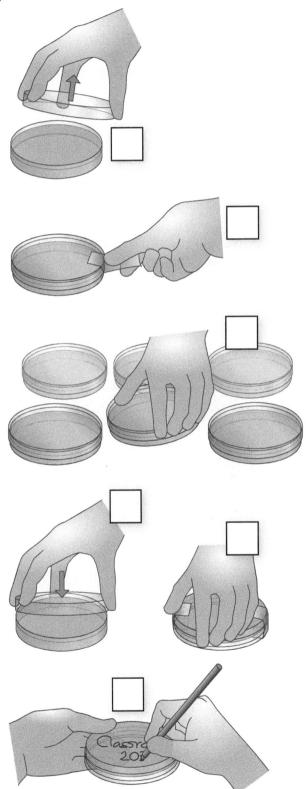

Jon needs to complete his experiment. He follows the instructions again, but this time he puts the dish into Classroom 204.

2 Which **variables** should Jon keep the same?
Tick **all** the correct ones.

the room where he puts the dish ☐

the type of jelly in the dish ☐

the length of time he leaves the lid off ☐

the type of pen he uses to label the dish ☐

The diagram shows the two dishes after they have been left in the laboratory for five days.

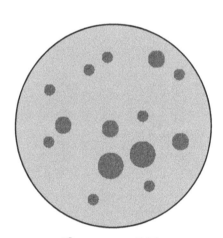

Classroom 203

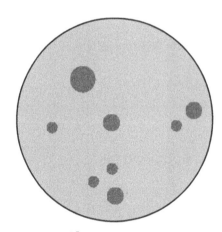

Classroom 204

3 Complete this conclusion that Jon can make from his experiment:

There are .... micro-organisms in the air in Classroom 203 than in Classroom 204.

2.2 Bread dough experiment

This exercise relates to **2.2 Micro-organisms** and **2.4 Micro-organisms and food** from the Coursebook.

> In this exercise, you think about variables again. You practise drawing results charts and making conclusions.

Nor does an experiment to answer this question:

Does bread dough rise more if you add more sugar?

Nor makes bread dough using flour, water, yeast and sugar.

She makes five different sets of dough.

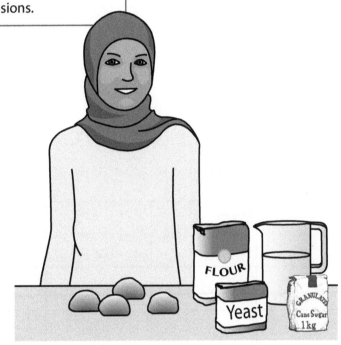

1 Which variable should Nor change in her five sets of dough? Which variables should she keep the same?
Tick **one** box in each row.

Variable	Change	Keep the same
the type of flour		
the mass of flour		
the mass of sugar		
the volume of water		
the temperature		

> **Remember**
>
> A row goes across a table.
>
> A column goes down a table.

Nor puts each piece of dough into a measuring cylinder.

She measures the volume at the start and after one hour. She makes her measurements in cm³.

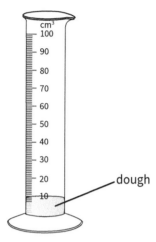

dough

Here is Nor's results table.

Mass of sugar in g	Volume of dough at start	Volume of dough after one hour	Increase in volume of dough
0	10.0	10.6	0.6
0.5	9.9	14.5	
1.0	10.1	18.3	
1.5	10.2	33.7	
2.0	10.0	48.6	

2 Something important is missing in three of the headings in Nor's results table.

What is missing? Add the missing words to the three headings.

3 Complete the last column in the results table.

4 Write a conclusion that Nor can make from the results of her experiment.

....

....

....

> **Remember**
>
> Look at the question that Nor's experiment was planned to answer.
>
> Use the question to help you to write the conclusion.

2.3 Drawing and labelling a plant cell

This exercise relates to **2.6 Plant cells** from the Coursebook.

In this exercise, you practise making and labelling a clear, simple diagram.

Amal makes a drawing of a plant cell.

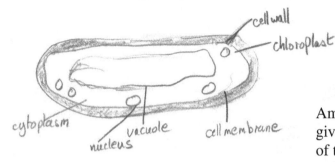

Amal's teacher gives him a list of three things to improve on his drawing.

- Make sure each label line touches the structure it is labelling.

- Take care to get the shapes and proportions correct.

- Do not shade or colour your drawing.

1 Write down **two** more ways that Amal can improve his labels.

....

....

....

....

2 Draw and label a better diagram of the same plant cell in the space below.

Remember

Look at exercise 1.1 if you have forgotten about labels.

2.4 Comparing plant cells and animal cells

This exercise relates to **2.6 Plant cells** and **2.7 Animal cells** from the Coursebook.

> In this exercise, you practise using a table to compare two things.

Anna draws a table to compare animal cells and plant cells.

Here is Anna's table, with one row filled in.

Animal cells	Plant cells
have a cell membrane	have a cell membrane

1 Write each of these statements in a suitable place in the table.

   Two of the statements need to be written twice, once in each column.

   have a cell wall

   have a nucleus

   have cytoplasm

   sometimes have chloroplasts

   do not have a cell wall

   never have chloroplasts

> ## Remember
>
> Write statements about the same feature in the same row.
>
> This makes it easy to compare the same feature in the two types of cell.

3.1 Adaptations of tigers

This exercise relates to **3.1 Adaptations** from the Coursebook.

> In this exercise, you choose suitable answers from a list. You also practise labelling a diagram carefully.

The diagram shows a tiger. Tigers are predators that hunt, kill and eat other animals.

The list shows some adaptations of different animals.

- **sharp claws for catching and holding prey**   • **strong legs for burrowing**

- **stripes for camouflage**   • **eyes at front of head to focus clearly on prey**

- **sharp, cutting teeth to kill prey**   • **webbed feet for swimming underwater**

- **eyes at side of head to see predators approaching**

- **smooth, streamlined body for reducing friction**

> **Remember**
>
> An adaptation is a feature that helps an organism to survive.

1. Choose from the list the **four** adaptations that a tiger has.

   Label the diagram of the tiger to show these adaptations.

2. Then think of **one** more adaptation. Add this to the labels on the diagram.

3.2 Drawing a food chain

This exercise relates to **3.2 Food chains** from the Coursebook.

In this exercise, you find information in some sentences.
You use the information to draw a food chain.

A food chain shows how energy passes from one living
organism to another, as the organisms eat each other.

Look at this example.

grass ⟶ zebra ⟶ lion

Here is information about another
food chain.

1 Use a **green** pencil to draw a circle
around the name of a plant in the
sentences on the right.

2 Use a **blue** pencil to underline
the names of the **three** animals.
(Underline each name only once.)

3 Which organism is a producer?

....

4 Which **three** organisms are consumers?

....

- Porcupines are animals that live in North
  America. They eat plants. One of their favourite
  foods is the leaves of clover plants.

- Mink are predators. They eat young porcupines.

- Great horned owls are also predators.
  They eat mink.

5 Draw a food chain that contains the four organisms. You do not
need to draw pictures – just write the names of the organisms.

Remember

Start on the left with the
name of the plant.

Then draw an arrow, pointing
to the right, from the plant
to the animal that eats it.

You should have four
organisms and three arrows
in your completed food chain.

3.3 Water pollution

This exercise relates to **3.4 Pollution** from the Coursebook.

> In this exercise, you practise finding information from a bar chart. You use the information to make a suggestion.

Anna and Nor count the numbers of water boatmen in three different ponds.

In each pond, they count the water boatmen in a $10\,m^2$ area.

They draw a bar chart to show their results.

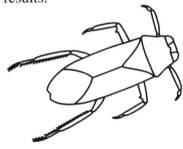

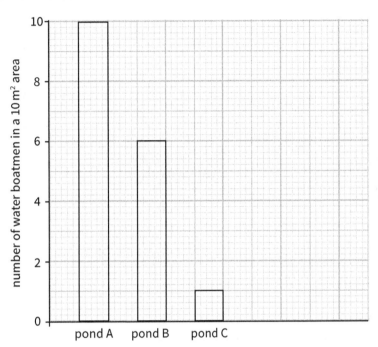

1 Which pond has one water boatman in $10\,m^2$?

   ....

2 How many water boatmen are there in $10\,m^2$ of pond B?

   ....

3 Which pond has an average of one water boatman in $1\,m^2$?

   ....

> **Remember**
>
> For question 3, remember that the numbers on the graph tell us how many water boatmen there are in $10\,m^2$.
>
> You need to work out how many there would be in $1\,m^2$.

4 Water boatmen like to live in unpolluted water.
   Suggest which pond is the **most** polluted.

   ....

   Explain your answer.

   ....

3.4 Air pollution

This exercise relates to **3.4 Pollution** from the Coursebook.

> In this exercise, you use information from a table to draw a bar chart. You then answer some questions about the information.

Polluted air often contains tiny particles of unpleasant substances, such as soot, in droplets of water. These are called particulate matter, or PM for short.

The table shows the level of PM pollution in the air of seven Asian cities in 2014.

City	PM pollution in micrograms per m^3
Delhi	150
Karachi	117
Dhaka	86
Beijing	56
Colombo	28
Jakarta	20
Singapore	17

1 Complete the bar chart on the next page to show this information.

> ### Remember
> You can use the heading from the table to label the y-axis.
>
> The y-axis is the one up the side of the graph.
>
> Use a pencil and ruler to draw the bars.
>
> Leave spaces between the bars for the different cities.
>
> Make sure the top of the bar is level and **exactly** at the correct height on the graph paper.
>
> Do not shade the bars.

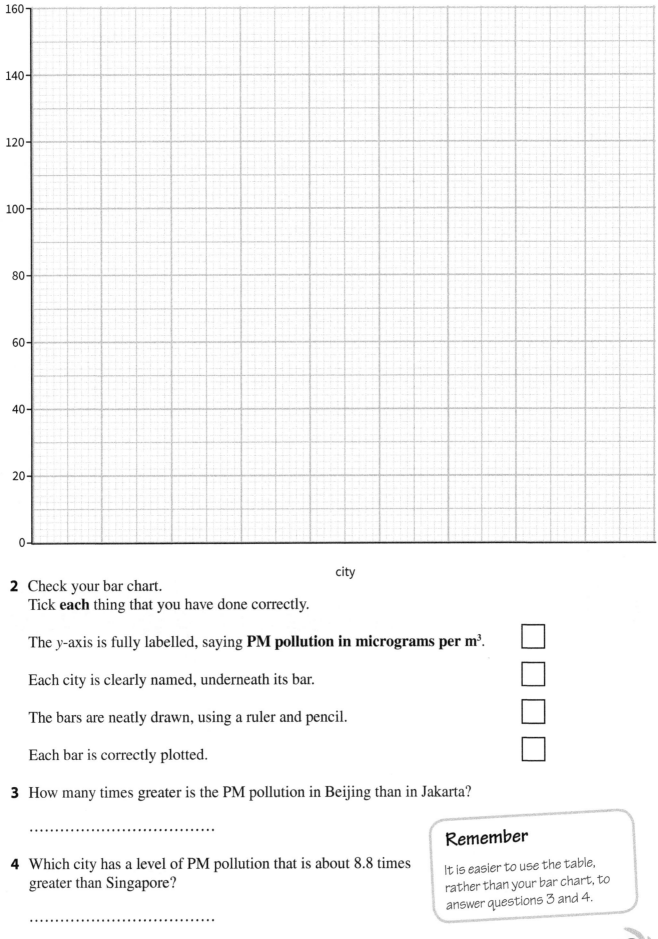

city

2 Check your bar chart.
Tick **each** thing that you have done correctly.

The *y*-axis is fully labelled, saying **PM pollution in micrograms per m³**. ☐

Each city is clearly named, underneath its bar. ☐

The bars are neatly drawn, using a ruler and pencil. ☐

Each bar is correctly plotted. ☐

3 How many times greater is the PM pollution in Beijing than in Jakarta?

....

4 Which city has a level of PM pollution that is about 8.8 times greater than Singapore?

....

> **Remember**
> It is easier to use the table, rather than your bar chart, to answer questions 3 and 4.

3.5 Conserving southern white rhinos

This exercise relates to **3.6 Conservation** from the Coursebook.

> In this exercise, you find information from a line graph.

Southern white rhinos live in Africa. They are an endangered species.

In the past, people shot rhinos for sport and to sell their horns.

Now, many people work hard to stop southern white rhinos from becoming extinct.

The graph shows the numbers of southern white rhinos in Africa from 1895 to 2012.

Remember

Look at the scales carefully.

One small square on the x-axis = two years.

One small square on the y-axis = 400 rhinos.

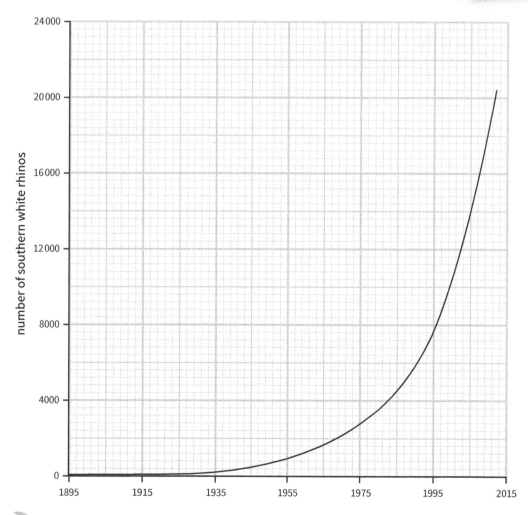

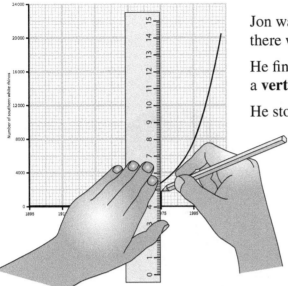

Jon wants to know how many rhinos there were in the year 1975.

He finds 1975 on the *x*-axis and draws a **vertical** line upwards, using a ruler.

He stops his line when it hits the curve.

Then he draws a **horizontal** line from this point, using a ruler, to the *y*-axis, like this.

1 Use Jon's work to find how many rhinos there were in the year 1975.

....

2 Follow Jon's example to find out how many rhinos there were in the year 2005.

Draw your lines on the big graph on the previous page.

....

3 Find the year in which there were 17200 rhinos. Draw your lines on the big graph again.

....

Remember

For question 3, you need to start on the *y*-axis.

Draw the horizontal line first.

Then draw the vertical line.

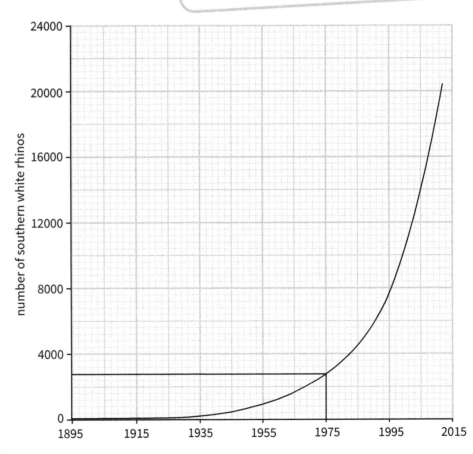

Unit 4 Variation and classification

4.1 Recording variation

This exercise relates to **4.2 Variation in a species** from the Coursebook.

> In this exercise, you practise completing a results table.
> Then you use your results table to draw a bar chart.

Amal's class has a garden outside the classroom.

Amal's teacher gives him some canna lily tubers to plant in the garden.

Amal and Sam plant the tubers. Each tuber grows into a plant and produces flowers.

The boys count the number of canna plants with different-coloured flowers.

Here is the table that they make.

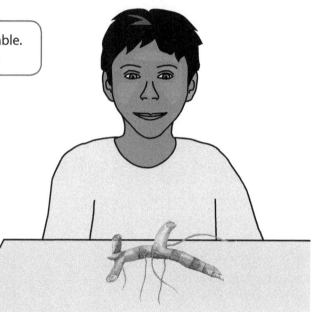

Flower colour	Yellow	White	Red	Orange
tally	ЖHT I	III	IIII	ЖHT II
number of plants				

1 Complete the last row of Amal's and Sam's results table.

2 Calculate the total number of canna plants.

   ....

3 Use Amal's and Sam's results table to draw a bar chart.

Put **flower colour** on the *x*-axis.

Put **number of plants** on the *y*-axis.

Remember

The x-axis is the one along the bottom of the graph.
The y-axis is the one up the side.

Use a pencil and ruler to draw your bar chart.

Leave spaces between the bars.

Do not shade the bars.

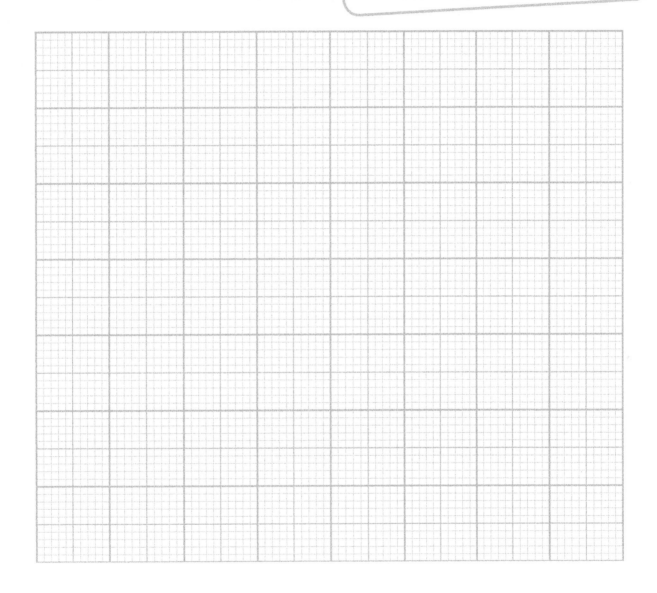

4 All canna lilies belong to the same species.

What word do we use to describe differences between individuals that belong to the same species?
Draw a circle around the correct answer.

adaptations   **features**   **frequency**   **variation**

4.2 Using a frequency diagram

This exercise relates to **4.3 Investigating variation** from the Coursebook.

> In this exercise, you find information from a frequency diagram.

Amal and Sam count the number of leaves on each of the canna plants in the class garden.

The boys use their results to draw a frequency diagram.

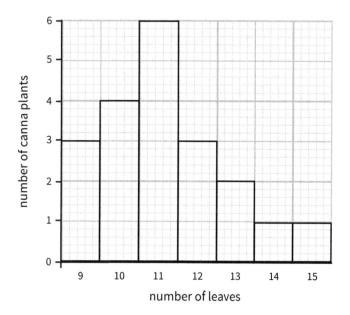

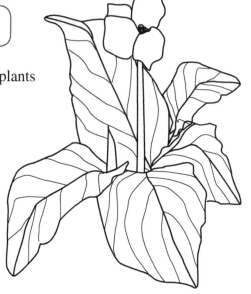

1 What is the smallest number of leaves on a canna plant?

....

2 How many plants have 12 leaves?

....

3 The most common value is called the **mode**.

What is the mode for the number of leaves on the canna plants?

.... leaves

4 The middle value is called the **median**.

What is the median for the number of leaves on the canna plants?

.... leaves

4.3 Constructing a frequency diagram

This exercise relates to **4.3 Investigating variation** from the Coursebook.

> In this exercise, you complete a results table. Then you use the results table to construct a frequency diagram.

Elsa and Nor count the number of flowers on each of the canna plants that Amal and Sam planted.

The girls write their results in a notebook.

```
Numbers of flowers on each plant:
   5   1   2   6    5
     3    7   4      5
  3    4   1   3    4
    2   5    3   4  4  2
```

1 How many plants are there?

   ....

2 Calculate the **mean** number of flowers on a canna plant.

   Show your working.

> **Remember**
>
> To find the mean, add up all the numbers of flowers.
>
> Then divide by the number of plants.

   ....

3 Use Elsa's and Nor's results to complete the results table.

Number of flowers on a plant	1	2					
Number of plants							

4 Use the results table to construct a frequency diagram.

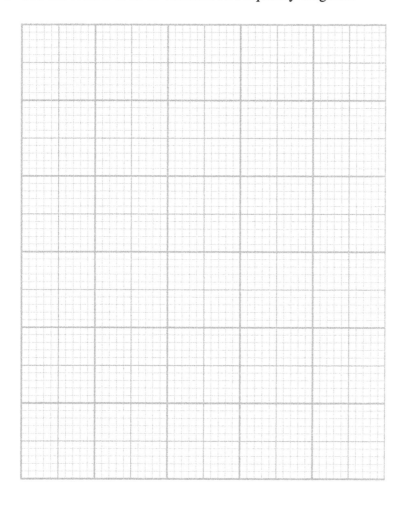

Remember

Put **number of flowers on a plant** on the x-axis.

Put **number of plants** on the y-axis.

Draw the bars neatly, all the same width.

Make the bars touch each other.

5 What is the mode for the number of flowers on the canna plants?

.... flowers

6 What is the median number of flowers on the canna plants?

.... flowers

7 Leaves and flowers are plant organs.

    a What is the function of leaves?

....

    b What is the function of flowers?

....

Unit 5 States of matter

5.1 Sorting solids, liquids and gases

This exercise relates to **5.1 States of matter** from the Coursebook.

> In this exercise, you draw a table and sort items into solids, liquids and gases.

Anna makes a cake for her family.

Here are the items she needs:

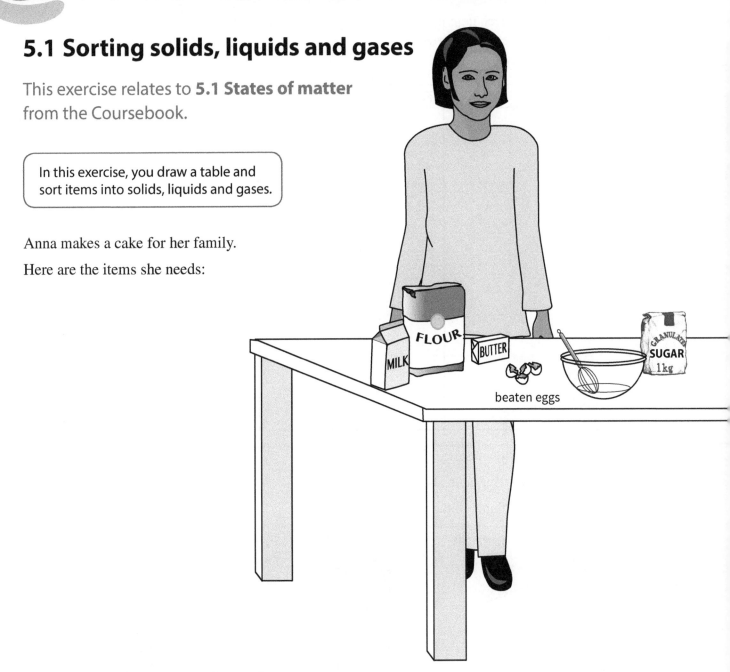

For the cake filling, Anna also needs:

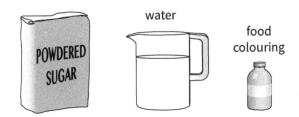

1 Write the names of each item pictured on the previous page, in the correct column of the table.

Solids	Liquids

2 Here are some different items.

Add their names to your table above.

You need to add a column to the table for gases.

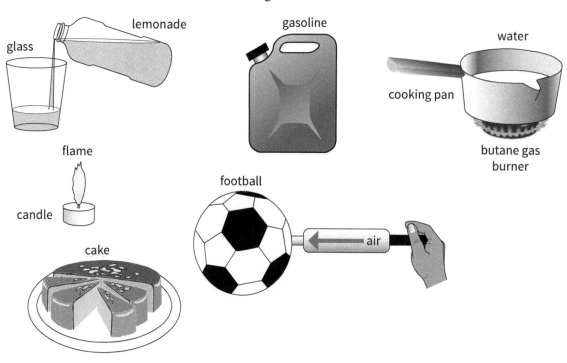

glass — lemonade — gasoline — water — cooking pan — butane gas burner — flame — candle — football — air — cake

5.2 Heating water

This exercise relates to **5.3 Changing state** from the Coursebook.

> In this exercise, you practise drawing a table and using it to record the results of an investigation.

Amal does an **investigation**.

He first takes the **temperature** of the water in the beaker (at 0 minutes).

Then he heats the water.

He takes the temperature every minute.

He does this for ten minutes.

1 Draw a table below for Amal to record his results.

> **Remember**
>
> Draw with a pencil and use a ruler.
>
> Put **Time in minutes** as a heading in the first column.
>
> Give the second column a heading with units.
>
> You need enough rows for all the results.

2 The diagrams show Amal's thermometer after different times. Write the temperature in the space.

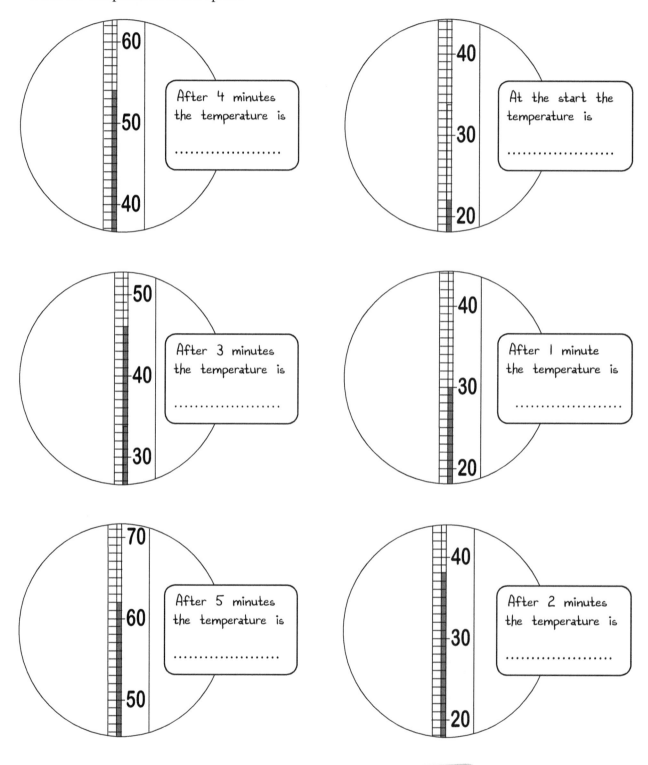

After 4 minutes the temperature is ....

At the start the temperature is ....

After 3 minutes the temperature is ....

After 1 minute the temperature is ....

After 5 minutes the temperature is ....

After 2 minutes the temperature is ....

3 Write the results into your table on the previous page.

Remember

The results need to be in order.

5.3 Plotting a graph

This exercise relates to **5.3 Changing state** from the Coursebook.

In this exercise, you draw a graph.

Remember

Use a pencil.

Find the time on the x-axis.

Go upwards until you come to the correct temperature.

Mark with a neat, small cross.

1 Use your table of results in exercise 5.2 to plot a graph.

First label the axes with the **units**: time in minutes and temperature in °C.

Then plot each point carefully. The first one has been done for you.

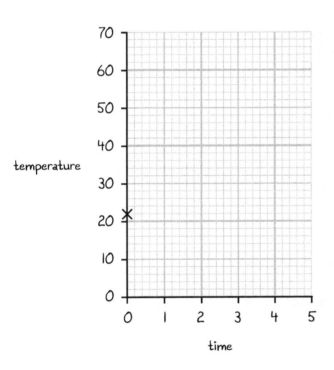

2 Look carefully at the points you have plotted.

Draw a smooth line to join the points.

3 Write a sentence to describe what the graph shows.

Remember

Use a pencil.

Look at all the points together.

Do they form a line? Can you use a ruler? Move the ruler so that the line goes through most of the points.

....

....

5.4 Particles in a solid

This exercise relates to **5.4 Explaining changes of state** from the Coursebook.

> In this exercise, you sort out facts about solids.

All matter is made up of particles. The diagram shows the particles in a solid.

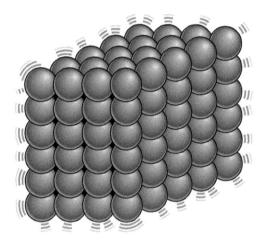

1 The statements below are about particles in a solid.
   Tick **each** statement that is correct.

The particles are arranged in a regular pattern. ☐	The particles are not arranged in a pattern. ☐
The particles can move to different places. ☐	The particles are in fixed positions. ☐
The particles can vibrate. ☐	The particles stay still. ☐
The particles do not touch each other. ☐	The particles are touching one another. ☐

This diagram shows what happens to the particles in a solid when it is heated.

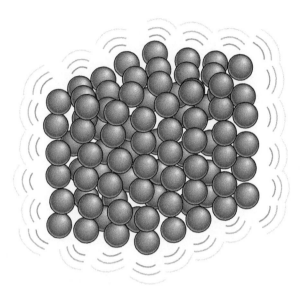

2 The statements below are about what happens to the particles when a solid is heated.
   Tick **each** statement that is correct.

When a solid is heated, heat energy is transferred **to** the particles. ☐

When a solid is heated, heat energy is transferred **from** the particles. ☐

The heat energy makes the particles vibrate more. ☐

The heat energy makes the particles vibrate less. ☐

Vibrating particles take up less space. ☐

Vibrating particles take up more space. ☐

The solid shrinks. ☐

The solid expands. ☐

6.1 Metal properties and uses

This exercise relates to **6.1 Metals** from the Coursebook.

> In this exercise, you match properties of metals to their uses.

1 Look at the drawings. Use them to help you complete the sentences.

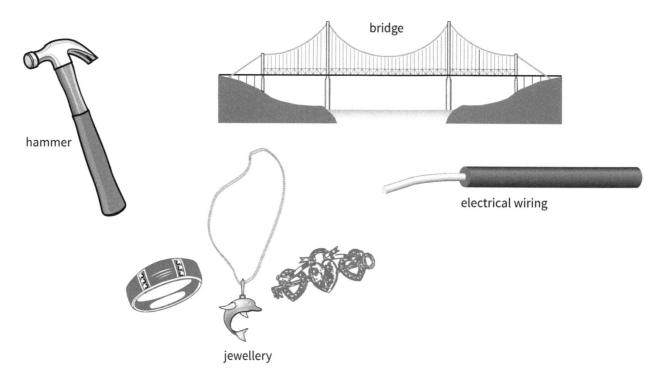

a Metals are strong and tough.

This is why iron is used for:

....

b Metals are usually shiny.

This is why gold is used for:

....

c Metals are good conductors of electricity.

This is why copper is used for:

....

6.2 Temperature scale

This exercise relates to **6.2 Non-metals** from the Coursebook.

> In this exercise, you practise using a temperature scale, including temperatures that are below 0 °C.

Some non-metals have melting points below 0 °C, and some also have boiling points below 0 °C.

The diagram below shows a temperature scale in degrees Celsius (°C).

The scale shows temperatures from 100 °C to −70 °C. A temperature of −70 °C means 70 °C **below** 0 °C.

Jon is having problems reading the temperature scale.

Remember

At 10 °C, water is liquid.

At −10 °C, water is solid (ice).

At 0 °C, ice melts.

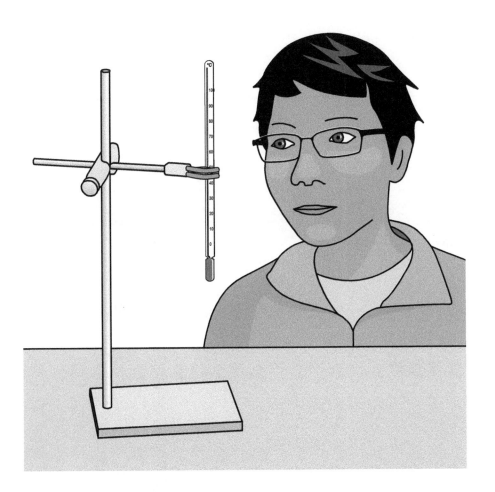

1 To help Jon, mark your answers on the scale.
The first one has been done for you.

   a Mark **A** at 30 °C on the scale.

   b Mark **B** at –30 °C on the scale.

   c Mark **C** at 0 °C on the scale.

2 The temperature is 0 °C and it gets 10 °C **warmer**.
Mark the new temperature as **D** on the temperature scale.

3 The temperature is 0 °C and it gets 10 °C **colder**.
Mark the new temperature as **E** on the scale.

4 What temperature is 20 °C **colder** than –50 °C?

   ....

5 Mark this temperature as **F** on the temperature scale.

6 What temperature is 20 °C **warmer** than –40 °C?

   ....

7 Mark this temperature as **G** on the scale.

6 Material properties

6.3 Metal or non-metal?

This exercise relates to **6.3 Comparing metals and non-metals** from the Coursebook.

> In this exercise, you sort metals and non-metals and plot a bar chart.

Nor has a list of metals and non-metals, mixed up.
She needs to sort them out.

1 Tick **each** answer in the table that Nor has correct.

Write the correct answer for any she has wrong.

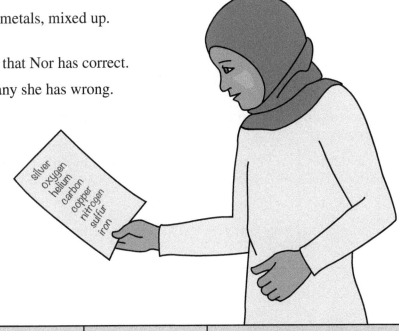

Remember

Think about the properties of metals and non-metals.

List of materials	Nor's answer	Correct?	Correct answer if Nor is wrong
silver	metal		
oxygen	non-metal		
helium	non-metal		
carbon	metal		
copper	metal		
nitrogen	non-metal		
sulfur	metal		
iron	metal		

2 How many metals does Nor think there are?

....

3 What is the correct number of metals?

....

4 How many non-metals does Nor think there are?

....

5 What is the correct number of non-metals?

....

Remember

Use a pencil and ruler to draw the bars.

Label the bars.

Do not shade the bars.

6 Use the correct numbers from questions 3 and 5 to complete the bar chart.

Bar chart of metals and non-metals

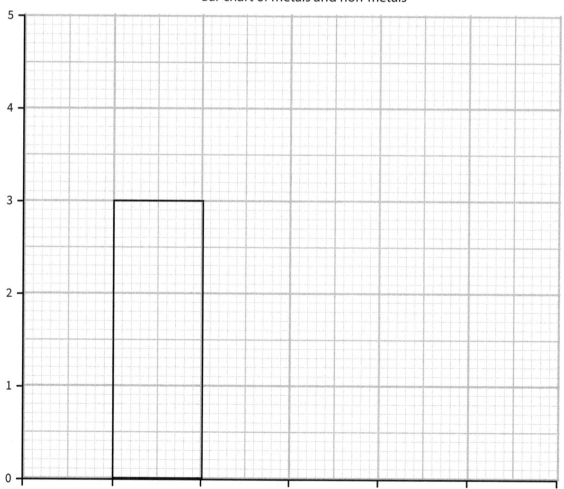

6.4 Different materials

This exercise relates to **6.4 Everyday materials and their properties** from the Coursebook.

> In this exercise, you make a tally chart and use it to plot a bar chart.

1 Look at the drawings. Each of the items is made of one of the materials in the tally chart on the next page.

Decide what the items are made from.

plastic toy ducks

exercise book

T shirt

ticket

business card

saucepan

paper plate

brass nut

lunch box

glass vase

nail

poster

gold necklace

stainless steel knife

plastic sandal

plastic soda bottle

baseball cap

window pane

Put tally marks in the correct row. The first one has been done for you.

Material	Tally
paper	|||||
plastic	
metal	
fibres	
glass	

Remember

Draw a mark for each item.

If you have a fifth item, draw a line across the other four marks.

If you have a sixth item, start another block.

2 Use the information from your tally chart to complete the bar chart.

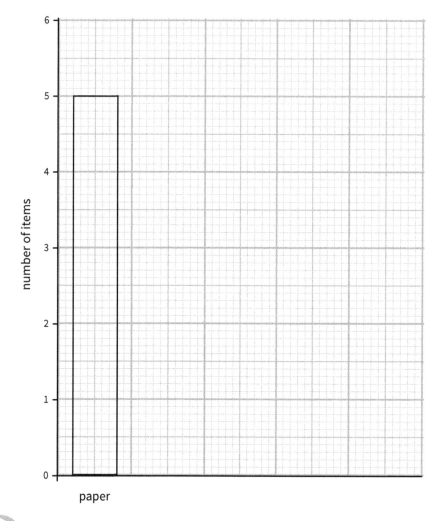

Remember

Leave a space between the bars.

Make the bars the same width.

Label each bar.

6.5 Choosing the correct word

This exercise relates to **6.4 Everyday materials and their properties** from the Coursebook.

In this exercise, you choose correct words and phrases.

Glass is a useful material. It is often used for containers for food and drink.

1 Draw a circle around the correct word (or words) in the sentences below.

Read the sentence and the hint carefully.

Look at this example.

Plastic is used for the outside of electrical plugs because
it is a good **conductor** / ⟨**insulator.**⟩

Hint: Choose the word that means it does not have electricity flowing through it.

a   Glass is used for containers for food and drink because it

is **opaque** / **transparent**.

Hint: Choose the word that means you can see the food or drink inside.

b   Glass is used because it **does not react** / **does react** with

the food or drink.

Hint: Choose the words that mean it does not change the food or drink.

c   Glass is used because it is **waterproof** / **porous**.

Hint: Choose the word that means it does not let the liquid out.

d   Glass is cheap to make and can be **thrown away** / **recycled**.

Hint: Choose the word or words that mean it can be made into other things.

7.1 Acid or alkali?

This exercise relates to **7.1 Acids and alkalis**, **7.2 Is it an acid or an alkali?** and **7.3 The pH scale** from the Coursebook.

> In this exercise, you use a table to sort facts about acids and alkalis.

> Foods that contain acids taste sharp.

> The pH scale measures how strong an acid or alkali is. The scale goes from 0 to 14. 0 is a very strong acid and 14 a very strong alkali.

1 Draw a table with two columns below.

Put the headings **Acid** in the first column and **Alkali** in the second column.

> **Remember**
>
> Use a pencil and a ruler.

2 Write these pieces of information about acids and alkalis in the correct column of the table.

Lemon juice has a sharp tangy taste.

pH 9

Sodium hydroxide

A purple colour with Universal Indicator solution

Hydrochloric acid turns litmus paper red.

Toothpaste

Vinegar

A yellow colour with Universal Indicator solution

7.2 Finding mistakes in a table

This exercise relates to **7.3 The pH scale** from the Coursebook.

> In this exercise, you check facts about acids and alkalis.

Sam tests some liquids with Universal Indicator solution.

1 Draw a circle around each mistake he makes in his results table.

Write the correct answer in the space below each circled mistake.

Liquid	Colour with Universal Indicator solution	pH	
lemon juice	yellow	4	weakly alkaline
soap solution	blue/green	8	weakly alkaline
water	green	5	neutral
hydrochloric acid	blue	2	strongly acid
sodium hydroxide	blue/purple	11	strongly alkaline

7.3 Measuring

This exercise relates to **7.4 Neutralisation** from the Coursebook.

> In this exercise, you practise reading measurements from measuring cylinders and burettes.

The diagrams show measuring cylinders with liquid in them.

1 Write the volume of liquid in each measuring cylinder.

One has been done for you, as an example.

> ### Remember
>
> The surface of the liquid is slightly curved. We call the curved surface the meniscus.
>
> The volume of liquid is measured from the bottom of the curve.
>
> Write the units.

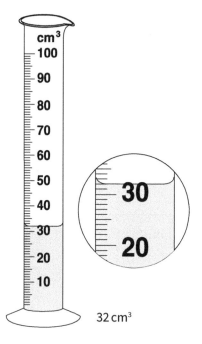

32 cm³

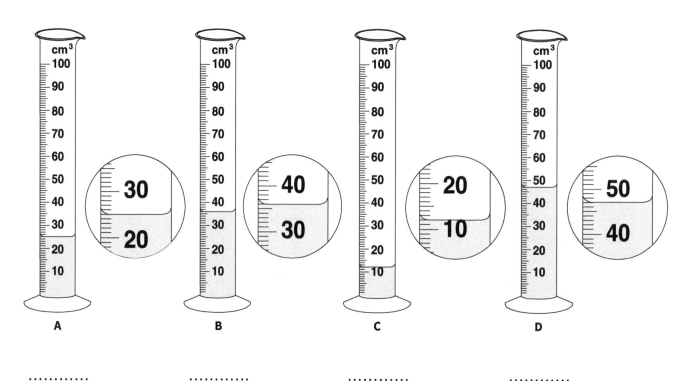

A ....

B ....

C ....

D ....

Diagrams A to D show burettes with no liquid in them.

2 Mark the level of the liquid at these volumes:

A 20 cm³

B 35 cm³

C 15 cm³

D 5 cm³

One has been done for you, as an example.

> ## Remember
>
> The surface of the liquid (meniscus) is slightly curved.
>
> The volume of liquid is measured from the bottom of the curve.
>
> The scale on a burette starts with zero at the top.

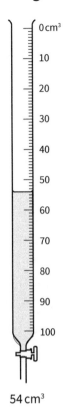

54 cm³

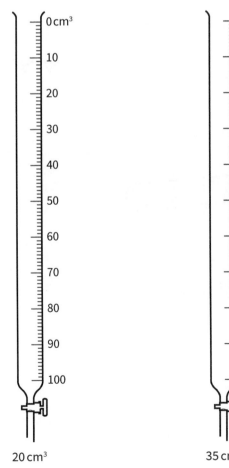

20 cm³

A

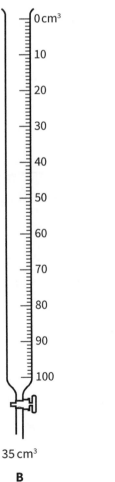

35 cm³

B

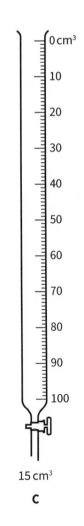

15 cm³

C

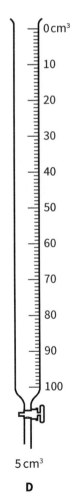

5 cm³

D

7.4 Testing soils

This exercise relates to **7.5 Neutralisation in action** from the Coursebook.

In this exercise, you sort the steps in an investigation into the correct order.

Nor and Elsa test soil to find out how acid or alkaline it is.

They have the instructions, but not in the correct order.

1 Write a number next to each diagram to show the order of each step.

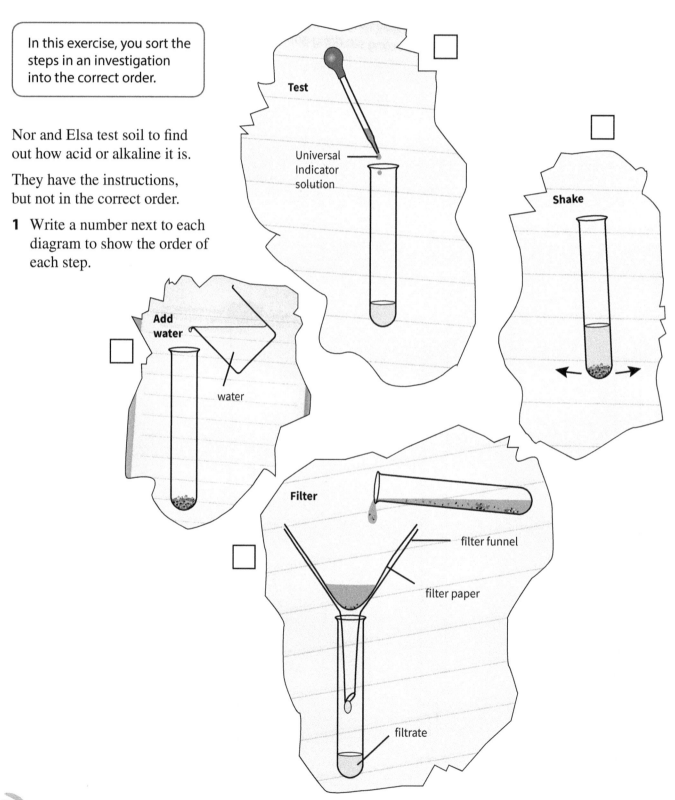

7.5 Indigestion investigation

This exercise relates to **7.6 Investigating acids and alkalis** from the Coursebook.

> In this exercise, you make sure that an investigation is a fair test.

When your stomach makes too much acid, you have indigestion.

You can take medicine to help this.

The medicine is an alkali and it neutralises the acid.

Amal and Anna test some indigestion medicines to see how well they work.

They find out how much of each medicine is needed to neutralise some acid.

They have three types of powder to test.

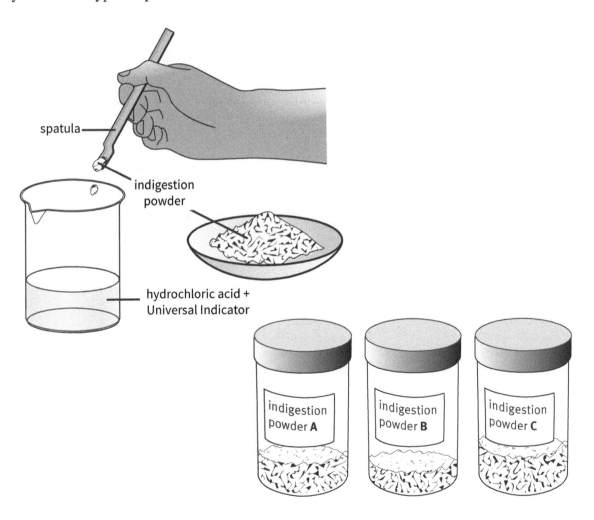

They watch for the acid plus Universal Indicator turning green.

They count the number of spatulas of each powder needed to do this.

This is their table to record the results.

1 Write a heading for the second column.

Powder	
A	
B	
C	

2 Other students in Amal's and Anna's class do some tests.

Look at the diagrams of what they do. Decide if each is a fair test, or not.

Under each set of diagrams write **fair** or **not fair**.

Sam's test

powder **A**

50 cm³ hydrochloric acid
and 3 drops of Universal
Indicator solution

powder **B**

25 cm³ hydrochloric acid
and 3 drops of Universal
Indicator solution

powder **C**

50 cm³ hydrochloric acid
and 3 drops of Universal
Indicator solution

....

Why do you think that?

....

....

Jon's test

powder **A**

powder **B**

powder **C**

50 cm³ sulfuric acid and 3 drops of Universal Indicator solution

50 cm³ hydrochloric acid and 3 drops of Universal Indicator solution

50 cm³ hydrochloric acid and 3 drops of Universal Indicator solution

....

Why do you think that?

....

....

Elsa's test

powder **A**

powder **B**

powder **C**

50 cm³ hydrochloric acid and 3 drops of Universal Indicator solution

50 cm³ hydrochloric acid and 3 drops of Universal Indicator solution

50 cm³ hydrochloric acid

....

Why do you think that?

....

....

8.1 Comparing different soils

This exercise relates to **8.1 Rocks, minerals and soils** from the Coursebook.

> In this exercise, you compare the structure and properties of different soils.

Soil is made up of small pieces of rock, mixed with humus. The pieces of rock may include sand and clay. Humus is the remains of plants and animals and their waste products.

The diagrams show some of the particles in two different soils.

Sandy soil

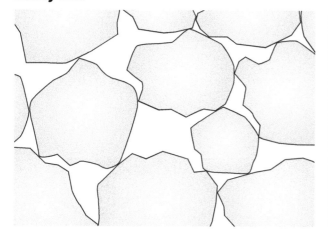

Clay soil

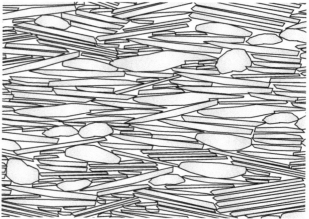

1 Draw a circle around the correct answer in **a** to **c**.

   a Which soil has larger particles? **sandy** or **clay**

   b Which soil has larger air spaces between the particles? **sandy** or **clay**

   c Which soil will hold water longer? **sandy** or **clay**

2 Read this information. Draw a circle around **one** of the words for each gap.

   When it rains the sandy soil will drain more **slowly / quickly**. This is because there

   are **large / small** air spaces between the sand particles. The water moves past the

   sand particles more **slowly / quickly**.

8.2 Investigating soil drainage

This exercise relates to **8.2 Soil** from the Coursebook.

> In this exercise, you help to plan an investigation.

Jon wants to investigate how quickly or slowly water drains through different types of soil. The diagram shows the apparatus.

These are Jon's instructions:

1. Place a measured volume of soil in the filter paper in the funnel.

2. Pour a measured volume of water onto the soil.

3. Collect the liquid that comes through in five minutes.

4. Repeat with different soils.

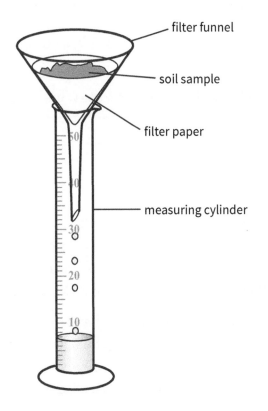

filter funnel

soil sample

filter paper

measuring cylinder

> **Remember**
>
> In an investigation you change **only one variable**.

1 What must Jon change in this investigation?

....

2 What things must Jon keep the same in this investigation?
Underline **all** the correct answers.

volume of soil   **volume of water added**   **time allowed for draining**

type of soil used   **volume of water collected**

3 Which other items of apparatus does Jon need to use in this investigation?
Underline **all** the correct answers.

stop clock   **top pan balance**   **a thermometer**

ruler   **a second measuring cylinder**

8.3 How igneous rocks are formed

This exercise relates to **8.3 Igneous rocks** from the Coursebook.

> In this exercise, you match some words about rocks to their meanings.

Read this information.

The crust of the Earth is made of solid rock. The inside of the Earth is very hot. When rock is very hot, it melts to form liquid. Beneath the crust the rock is molten (hot and liquid). The molten rock is called magma.

When magma reaches the Earth's surface it is called lava. The lava erupts from volcanoes. When lava and magma cool, they solidify and form rocks. Rocks formed like this are called igneous rocks.

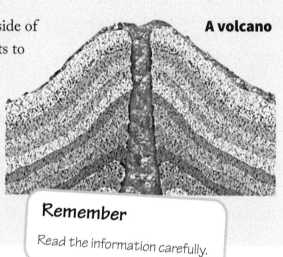

A volcano

Remember

Read the information carefully.

1 Use the information above to answer these questions .

   a Which word means **changes from a solid to a liquid**?

   ....

   b Which word means **the outer layer of the Earth**?

   ....

   c Which **two** words **describe magma**?

   ....

   d Which word means **magma that comes out of a volcano**?

   ....

   e Which word means the rock is **hot and liquid**?

   ....

8.4 True or false?

This exercise relates to **8.4 Sedimentary rocks** from the Coursebook.

In this exercise, you decide if facts about sedimentary rocks are true or false.

Read this information and look at the diagram.

Sedimentary rocks are formed when layers of fragments of rocks or mud collect on the seabed. As more layers build up, the weight of the new layers presses the particles or grains in the deeper layers together. Solid sedimentary rock is formed. Sometimes the remains of dead plants and animals fall into the sediment and become part of the rock. They may form fossils.

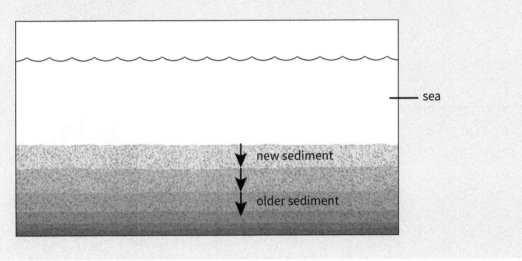

1 Write **true** or **false** next to each statement about sedimentary rocks.
Use the information above.

   a Sedimentary rocks never contain fossils. ....

   b Sedimentary rocks are formed in layers. ....

   c Sedimentary rocks are formed when volcanoes erupt. ....

   d Sedimentary rocks are formed in the sea. ....

   e Sedimentary rocks are formed of grains or particles that have been squeezed together.

   ....

8.5 Comparing rocks

This exercise relates to **8.3 Igneous rocks** and **8.4 Sedimentary rocks** from the Coursebook.

> In this exercise, you draw a table to compare igneous and sedimentary rocks.

1 Draw a large table with two columns below. Put the heading **Igneous** in the first column and the heading **Sedimentary** in the second.

Use a ruler and pencil.

Follow the instructions.

2 Write each of these words or phrases in the correct column of your table.
Make sure you use all the words. Tick them off as you write them in your table.

contains fossils	☐	**grains**	☐	**sandstone**	☐
formed from magma	☐	**lava**	☐	**molten rock**	☐
limestone	☐	**formed in the sea**	☐	**volcano**	☐
granite	☐	**has layers**	☐		
crystals	☐	**porous**	☐		

8.6 Investigating rocks

This exercise relates to **8.3 Igneous rocks**, **8.4 Sedimentary rocks** and
8.5 Metamorphic rocks from the Coursebook.

> In this exercise, you read the steps in an investigation,
> make a prediction and make a conclusion from the results.

Anna and Jon test some rock samples to see if they are porous.

This is their method:

> **Remember**
>
> Porous means it allows water to pass into it.

Find the mass of each rock.

Record the mass in a table.

Soak each rock in water for five minutes.

Dry the water from the outside of the rock,
then find the new mass.

Record the new mass in the table.

1 Make a prediction. Draw a circle round your chosen word in this sentence.

If a rock is porous, after soaking in water the mass will **stay the same / increase / decrease**.

Here are Anna's and Jon's results.

Rock sample	Mass at start in g	Mass after soaking in g
A	268	279
B	201	210
C	198	198
D	310	342

2 Look at the results table. Which samples are porous?

....

3 How much mass does sample A gain?

....

4 Which sample has the same mass after soaking in water?

....

5 The rocks Anna and Jon used do not all have the same mass.
Why does this **not** matter in this investigation?

....

8.7 Chemical weathering

This exercise relates to **8.6 Weathering** from the Coursebook.

> In this exercise, you find some mistakes in a results table and plot a graph.

Some rocks, such as limestone, are damaged by rain. Rain is slightly acidic. The acid reacts with the rock.

Amal and Sam investigate how acids of different pH affect limestone rocks.

They find the mass of the rocks before they start.

Then they put the rocks into the same volume of acid.

They check the mass of the rocks each day, until a rock's mass is half its mass at the start.

Here are the results. Look carefully at the table. Amal and Sam have made some mistakes in the way they have recorded their results.

> **Remember**
>
> Think about the order of the table and the units Sam and Amal should use.

pH of acid	Time for the mass to half
6	17
2	1 week
4	12
5	14
3	1 week and 3 days
1	3

1 Fill in this blank table to show the results correctly.

2 Use the results to plot a graph.

Put **pH** along the *x*-axis, and **Time** along the *y*-axis.

Make a small cross when you plot each point.

Remember

The x-axis is the one along the bottom of the graph. The y-axis is the one up the side. Check the scale carefully.

3 What do the results show?

....

8.8 Inside the Earth

This exercise relates to **8.10 The structure and age of the Earth** from the Coursebook.

> In this exercise, you label a diagram of the Earth. Then you answer questions about the parts of the Earth.

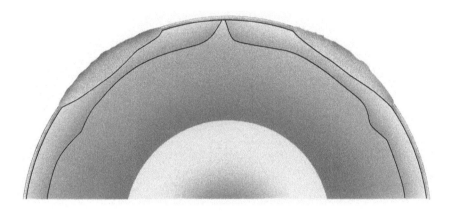

Remember

Use a ruler and pencil to draw your label lines.

Make sure the end of the label line touches the part you are labelling.

Make sure you do not write on the diagram.

Keep your writing horizontal.

1 Label the parts of the Earth shown in the diagram. Write these labels:

crust   **inner core**   **mantle**   **outer core**

2 Write which parts of the Earth are made of:

a the metals iron and nickel

....

b solid rock

....

c molten (hot liquid) rock or metal

....

d solid iron and nickel

....

e molten rock

....

9.1 Forces in pictures

This exercise relates to **9.1 Seeing forces** from the Coursebook.

> In this exercise, you draw arrows to show forces.

This is how force arrows are used:

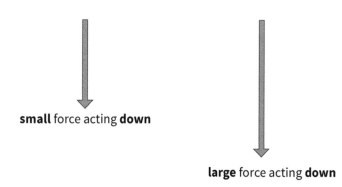

small force acting **down**

large force acting **down**

> **Remember**
>
> The **length** of the arrow shows the **size** of the force.
>
> The **direction** of the arrow shows the **direction** of the force.
>
> The arrows are **always straight** so draw them with a ruler.

Look at this example.

Nor is trying to lift her suitcase.

The arrow shows the force of Nor **pulling** up on the handle.

Her suitcase does **not** come off the ground.

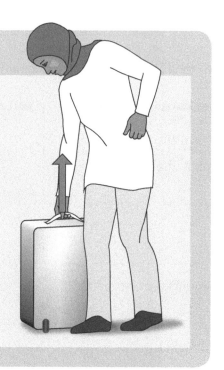

1 Nor tries again to lift her suitcase. This time she pulls up with a bigger force.

   Draw an arrow to show the bigger pulling force.

2 Sam is pushing his baby brother.

   Draw an arrow to show the **direction** of Sam's pushing force.

9.2 Weight arrows

This exercise relates to **9.3 Weight – the pull of gravity** from the Coursebook.

> In this exercise, you practise drawing force arrows to show the weight of an object.

Weight is a force. It pulls objects in the direction of gravity.

In most diagrams, weight will be an arrow pointing **down**.

The heavier an object, the greater its weight.

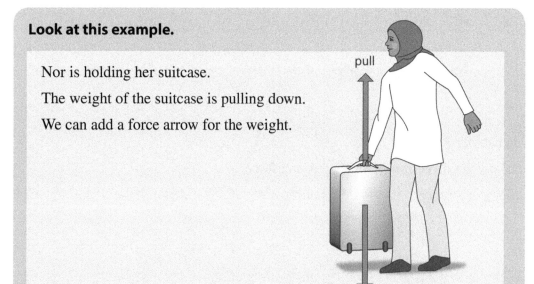

Look at this example.

Nor is holding her suitcase.

The weight of the suitcase is pulling down.

We can add a force arrow for the weight.

pull

weight

Nor carries her heavy suitcase and a lighter bag.

1 Draw **one** arrow to show the weight of the suitcase.

2 Draw **one more** arrow to show the weight of the lighter bag.

> **Remember**
>
> The length of the force arrow shows the size of the force.
>
> Use a ruler.

In some diagrams, the arrow for weight does **not** point straight down.

This is because gravity acts towards the centre of the Earth.

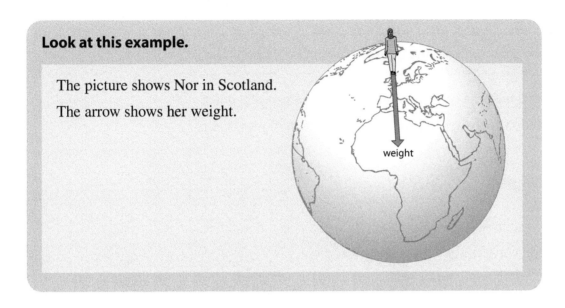

Look at this example.

The picture shows Nor in Scotland.

The arrow shows her weight.

weight

Nor goes to South Africa.

3 Draw an arrow to show her weight in South Africa.

Remember

Think about the **direction** and the **size** of the force.

9.3 Friction arrows

This exercise relates to **9.4 Friction – an important force** from the Coursebook.

In this exercise, you draw arrows to show the direction of the friction force.

Friction is a force that happens when two surfaces rub against each other.

The direction of friction is **always opposite** to the direction of movement.

Look at this example.

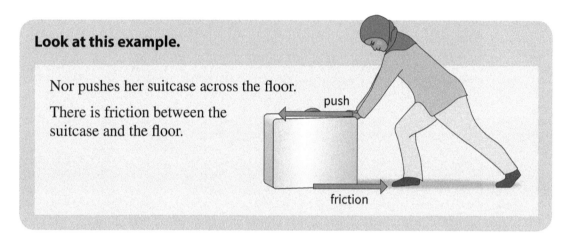

Nor pushes her suitcase across the floor.

There is friction between the suitcase and the floor.

1 Jon is pushing his desk across the floor.

Draw and label **one** arrow to show the **push** from Jon.

2 Jon finds it hard to push because of **friction**.

Draw and label **another** arrow to show how the friction acts.

Remember

Friction happens where two surfaces are in contact.

3 The brick is sliding down the ramp.

Draw an arrow to show the friction force.

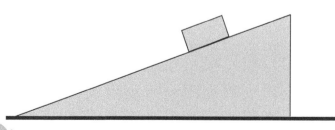

Remember

Friction always acts in the opposite direction to movement. Think about the direction the brick is going in.

9.4 Investigating friction

This exercise relates to **9.4 Friction – an important force** from the Coursebook.

In this exercise, you plan an investigation to answer the question:

How does the weight of an object affect the friction with a surface?

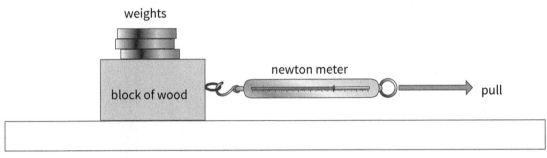

In investigations we change some things. These are called **variables**.

In a **fair test** you must change just **one** variable. You keep other variables the same.

1 Which of these variables must you keep the same?
Tick the boxes.

size of the block of wood ☐

size of the pull ☐

type of surface ☐

slope of the surface ☐

number of weights on the block ☐

angle of the pull ☐

> **Remember**
>
> First THINK:
> • You want to see how **weight** affects friction.
>
> Then ASK:
> • Will any of the other variables affect friction?
>
> Then DECIDE:
> • If it will affect friction, keep it the same.

9.5 The effect of air resistance

This exercise relates to **9.5 Air resistance** from the Coursebook.

> In this exercise, you draw arrows to show the direction of air resistance.

Air resistance is a force that is like friction but comes from the air.

1 Anna goes for a parachute jump.

   Her weight pulls her **down** through the air.

   Air resistance acts **up** on the parachute.

   Draw an arrow to show the air resistance.

weight

2 Sam drops a basketball.

   Draw an arrow to show the direction of air resistance on the ball as it falls.

> **Remember**
>
> The direction of air resistance is **always opposite** to movement.

3 The bus is moving along the road.

   Draw an arrow to show the air resistance.

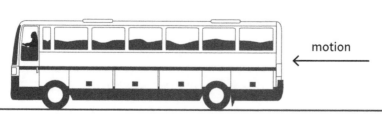

motion

10.1 Investigating energy

This exercise relates to **10.2 Chemical stores of energy** from the Coursebook.

> In this exercise, you learn how we can measure energy. You also draw a bar chart.

The energy in food can be measured by burning it.

The heat energy from burning can be used to heat water.

Nor weighs 5 g of some different foods.

She burns each of them in turn.

She records how much the temperature of the water goes up.

The more the temperature of the water goes up, the more energy in the food.

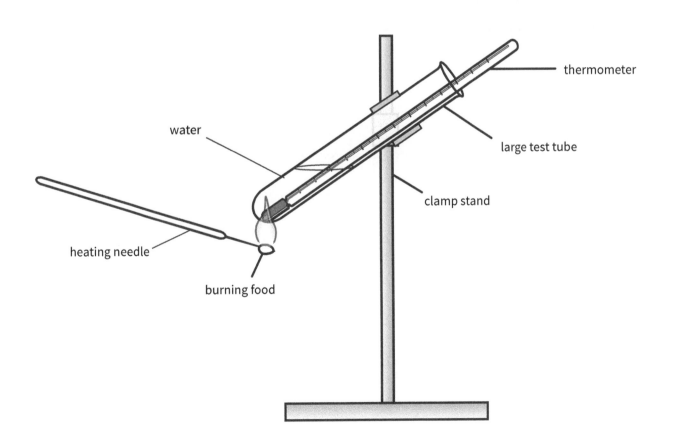

Nor uses the **same volume of water** for each type of food that is burned.

1 Why does she do this?
Tick **one** box.

to make it a fair test ☐

to make the food burn hotter ☐

to make the thermometer work ☐

Nor writes her results in a table.

Type of food	Temperature rise in °C
bread	20
cookie	45
cornflakes	27
pastry	41
wafer	32

Remember

Use a pencil and ruler to draw the bars.

Make all the bars the same width.

The bars should not be touching each other.

Make sure the top of the bar is level and exactly on the correct line of the graph paper.

Do not shade the bars.

2 Draw a bar chart of Nor's results.

The first bar has been drawn for you.

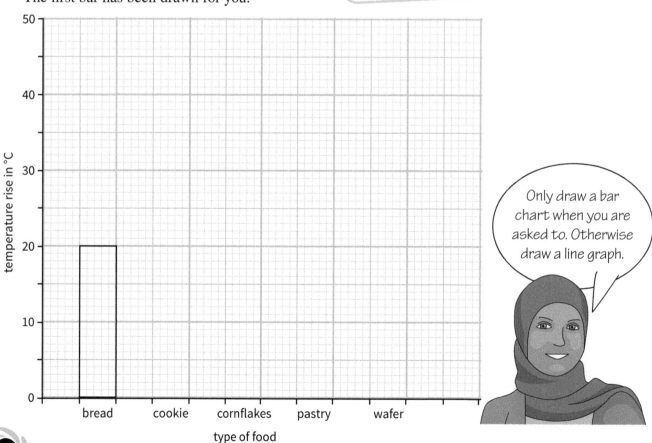

Only draw a bar chart when you are asked to. Otherwise draw a line graph.

10.2 Energy types

This exercise relates to **10.3 More energy stores**, **10.4 Thermal energy**, **10.5 Kinetic energy** and **10.6 Energy on the move** from the Coursebook.

> In this exercise, you match pictures to the types of energy.

1 Draw a line between each picture and the type of energy it shows.

Type of energy stored

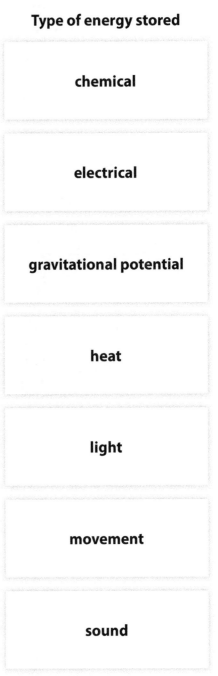

chemical

electrical

gravitational potential

heat

light

movement

sound

2 Sam does weightlifting.

He has cereal for breakfast before a competition.

What type of energy does the cereal contain?

Choose from the list in question 1.

....

3 Sam lifts the weights and holds them as high as he can.

What type of energy do the weights have when they have been lifted?

....

4 Sam then accidentally drops the weights down in front of him.

What type of energy do the weights have as they are falling?

....

5 When the weights hit the floor, there is a loud noise.

What type of energy is the loud noise?

....

10.3 Energy transfers

This exercise relates to **10.7 Energy changing form** from the Coursebook.

> In this exercise, you decide how energy is transferred.

Everything needs energy to work. Energy is transferred in different ways.

Here are some energy types, or forms:

chemical   electrical   heat   movement

gravitational   potential   light   sound

Look at this example.

Jon turns on the electric light in his room.

Electrical energy transfers to **light** energy.

The lamp also gets **hot**, so some of the electrical energy is transferred as **heat**.

Jon now turns the television on.

1 Complete the sentences using the forms of energy listed on this page.

The TV works using.........................energy.

We can see the picture because energy is transferred as ....

We can hear it because energy is transferred as ....

The television gets warm. This means some of the energy is transferred

as......................... .

10.4 Energy arrows

This exercise relates to **10.8 Energy is conserved** from the Coursebook.

> In this exercise, you learn how arrows can be used to show **how much** energy is transferred.

The rule about energy is:

> Energy cannot be created or destroyed. It is always conserved.

This law means **three** things:

- It is **not** possible to make energy.
- It is **not** possible to get rid of energy.
- Energy can go into another form, but the amount of it always **stays the same**.

Look at this example.

In exercise 10.3, Jon turns on the electric light in his room.

This energy arrow shows how the energy is transferred. The **thicker** the arrow, the **more** energy is transferred.

200 J each second

20 J used as light

180 J spreads out as heat

---

1 Look at the energy arrow for the electric light above.

How does **most** of the electrical energy get transferred?

....

2 How did you decide on your answer to question 1?

....

3 What happens to the rest of the electrical energy?

....

Unit 11 The Earth and beyond

11.1 The Sun in the daytime

This exercise relates to **11.1 Day and night** from the Coursebook.

> In this exercise, you learn how the Sun appears to move across the sky.

1 Each morning, where does the Sun rise?
Tick **one** box.

in the north ☐

in the south ☐

in the east ☐

in the west ☐

Elsa records the position of the Sun in the sky in **one day**.

She does this at three different times:

- early morning
- midday
- late afternoon.

This is Elsa's drawing of her results.

Elsa's labelling is not finished.

2 Put the letter **W** to show **west** on her drawing.

3 Put the letter **M** in the Sun to show where it was at **midday**.

4 Put the letter **L** in the Sun to show where it was in the **late afternoon**.

11.2 What causes day and night?

This exercise relates to **11.1 Day and night** from the Coursebook.

In this exercise, you practise answering questions about the Earth's movement.

The Earth's axis is like a straight line from the North to the South Pole, through the middle of the Earth.

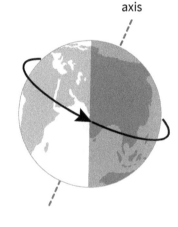

axis

1 How long does it take for the Earth to spin **once** on its axis? Tick **one** box.

one day ☐

one week ☐

one month ☐

one year ☐

Remember

The Earth spins on its axis.

This is what makes the Sun **appear** to move across the sky during the day.

This diagram shows the Earth, seen from space above the North Pole.

It shows how the Earth spins on its axis. The curved arrows show the direction that the Earth spins.

The diagram of the Earth also shows the direction of light from the Sun.

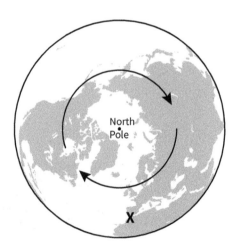

light from the Sun

North Pole

X

2 Shade **half** of the Earth in this diagram to show where it is **night**.

3 Put the letter **M** on the Earth to show where it is **midday**.

4 Draw a circle around the correct word at the end of this sentence:

The place **X** is just about to have **sunrise / sunset**.

11.3 Objects in the sky

This exercise relates to **11.4 Seeing stars and planets** from the Coursebook.

> In this exercise, you compare objects in the night sky.

The Sun and the other stars give out their own light.

The Moon and the planets **reflect** the light of the Sun. They do **not** give out their own light.

The Sun gives out light. Some of this light is reflected off the planets. That is how we can see the planets.

1 Draw lines on the diagram to show how light from the Sun reflects off the planet and then goes to Amal's eyes.

> **Remember**
>
> Light travels in straight lines.

Sun

planet

Amal

2 The Sun is a **star**. Why does it look bigger and brighter than other stars? Tick **one** box.

The Sun is the biggest star in our galaxy. ☐

The Sun is the brightest star in our galaxy. ☐

The Sun is the closest star to Earth. ☐

3 Amal wants to look at the planet Saturn.

Which piece of equipment can he use?
Tick **one** box.

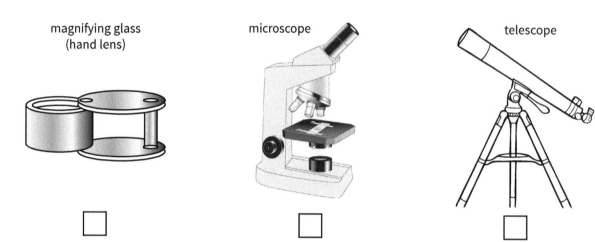

magnifying glass
(hand lens)

microscope

telescope

☐

☐

☐

4 Why must Amal **not** look directly at the Sun with **any** type of equipment?

....

5 Which of these objects give out their own light?
Tick **two** boxes.

Earth ☐

Jupiter (a planet) ☐

Moon ☐

Sirius (a star) ☐

Sun ☐

11.4 What is the Solar System?

This exercise relates to **11.6 A revolution in astronomy** from the Coursebook.

In this exercise, you learn about the movement of the planets.

The Earth we live on is one of the planets. The Earth, seven other planets and the Sun make up the Solar System.

A very long time ago, people believed the Earth was the centre of the Solar System.

They drew diagrams like this.

Remember

The Moon is not a planet.

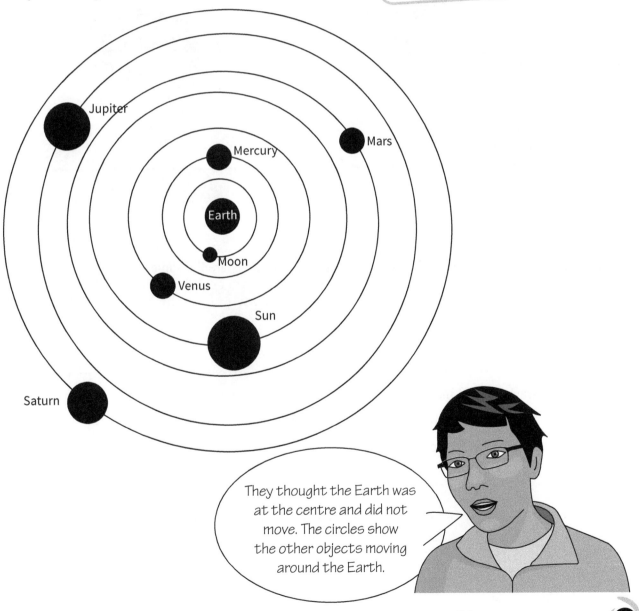

They thought the Earth was at the centre and did not move. The circles show the other objects moving around the Earth.

About 500 years ago, a man called Copernicus had a new idea.
His new idea fitted better with the way we can see the planets moving.

His diagram looked like this.

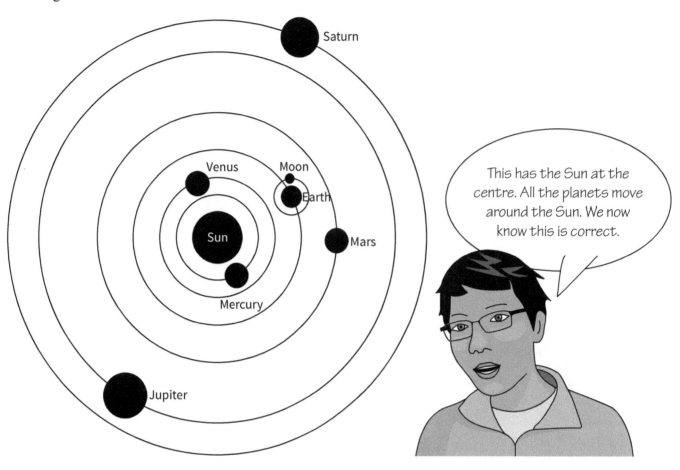

This has the Sun at the centre. All the planets move around the Sun. We now know this is correct.

1 Compare the two diagrams of the Solar System. Which things are the same in both?

....

....

....

2 The two diagrams do **not** include the planets Uranus or Neptune.

Uranus and Neptune are further away from the Sun than Saturn.

Suggest why these planets were **not** part of these early ideas.

....

....

....